NATIVE AMERICAN STYLE SEED BEAD JEWELRY

PART I
BRACELETS

48
LOOM PATTERNS

Copyright © 2016 Artium Studia
All rights reserved. No part of this book may be reproduced or transmitted in any form or by electronic or mechanical means, including information storage and retrieval systems, without permission in writing from the author.
For any questions, suggestions and comments, please contact at
http://www.etsy.com/shop/ArtiumStudia
artiumstudia@gmail.com

CONTENT

3 RACELETS

FOR EVERY PROJECT YOU WILL NEED:

- Seed beads: Czech (10°,15°) or Japanese (11°, 15°) seed beads
- Warp threads: cotton/embroidery/beading threads
- Weft thread: beading thread
- Beading needles: #10-12
- Bead loom
- Eyelet pliers (for several projects)

RECOMMENDED MATERIALS:

- Seed beads: Preciosa/Matsuno/Toho/Miyuki
- Cotton thread: DMC Petra 8 thread
- Embroidery threads: DMC threads
- Beading thread: Nymo/S-Lon

TIPS

- Suggested length of the warp threads for the bracelets with braids: 24"/60 cm; for the bracelets with leather bars: 18"/46 cm
- Use beading thread, size D with 10° seed beads
- Use beading thread, size OO/AA with 15° seed beads

3 BRACELETS

BRACELET #1
Length: 6.3"/16 cm
Width: 0.6"/1.4 cm

Materials:
- 8 warp threads (embroidery threads)
- 10° seed beads:
    3 g deep blue
    1 g white
    1 g yellow
    1 g red

BRACELET #2
Length: 6.3"/16 cm
Width: 0.6"/1.4 cm

Materials:
- 8 warp threads (cotton thread)
- 10° seed beads:
    3 g blue
    1 g black
    1 g yellow
    1 g red

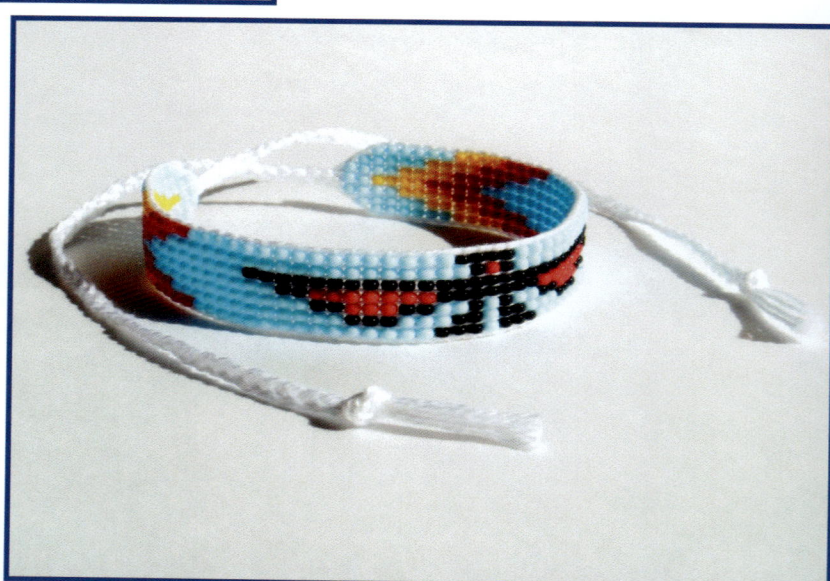

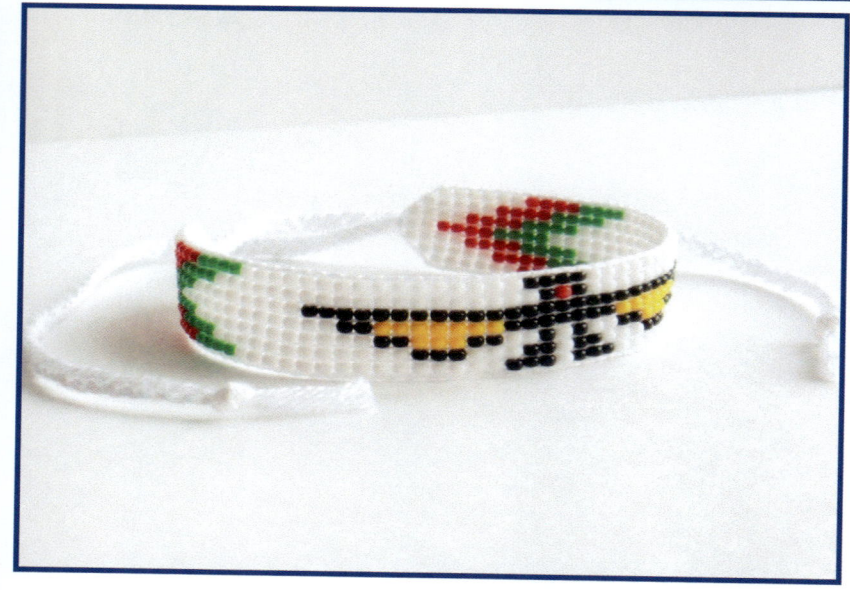

BRACELET #3
Length: 6.3"/16 cm
Width: 0.6"/1.4 cm

Materials:
- 8 warp threads (cotton thread)
- 10° seed beads:
    3 g white
    1 g black
    1 g green
    1 g yellow
    1 g red

5

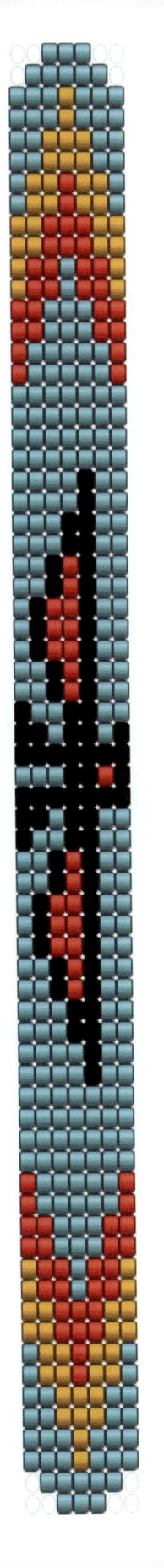

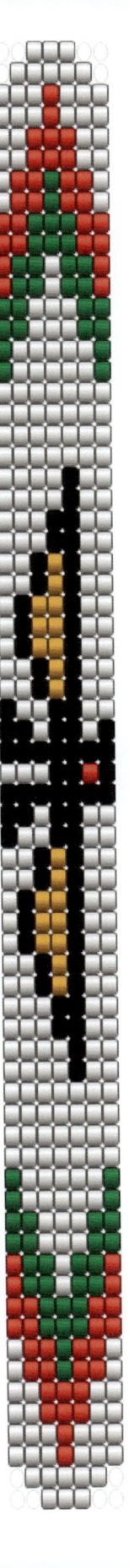

BRACELET #4
Length: 6.3"/16 cm
Width: 0.6"/1.4 cm

Materials:
- 8 warp threads (cotton thread)
- 10° seed beads:
  - 3 g black
  - 1 g white
  - 1 g yellow
  - 1 g red

BRACELET #5
Length: 6.3"/16 cm
Width: 0.6"/1.4 cm

Materials:
- 8 warp threads (cotton thread)
- 10° seed beads:
  - 3 g grey silver lined
  - 1 g white
  - 1 g light yellow
  - 1 g yellow
  - 1 g orange
  - 1 g red

BRACELET #6
Length: 6.3"/16 cm
Width: 0.6"/1.4 cm

Materials:
- 8 warp threads (cotton thread)
- 10° seed beads:
  - 3 g crystal silver lined
  - 1 g black
  - 1 g yellow
  - 1 g red

7

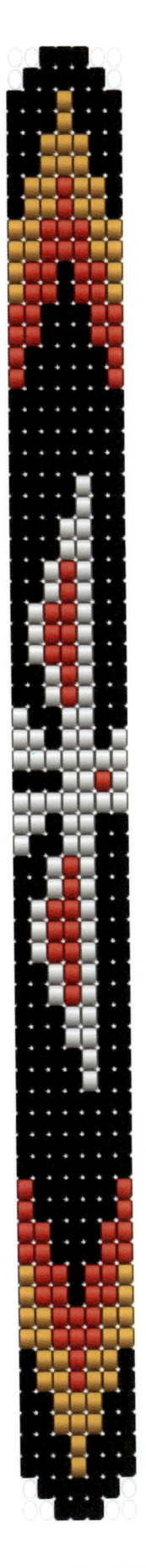

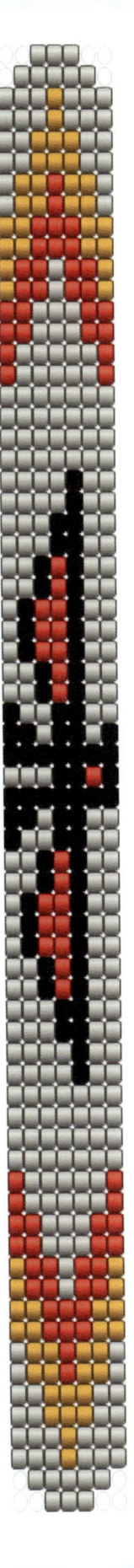

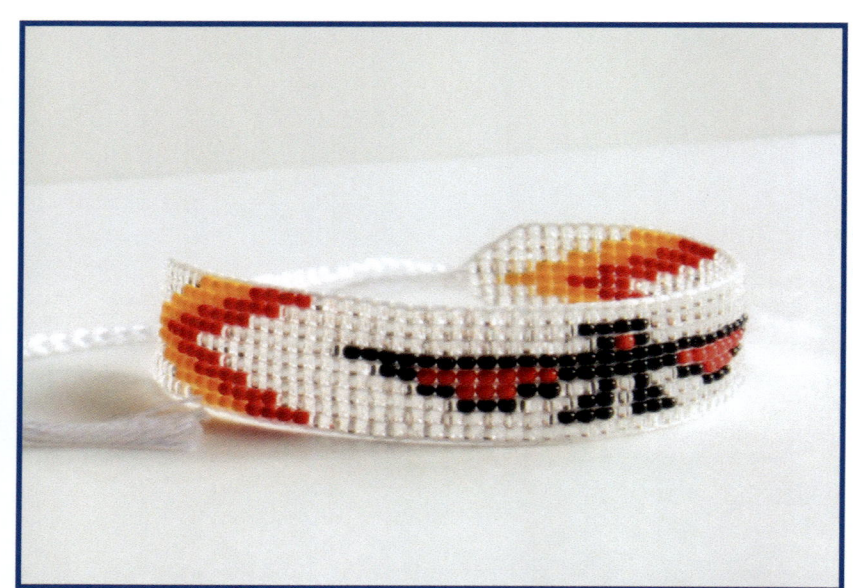

BRACELET #7
Length: 16"/6.3 cm
Width: 1.7"/0.7 cm

Materials:
- 10 warp threads (cotton thread)
- 10° seed beads:
    - 4 g crystal silver lined
    - 1 g black
    - 1 g yellow
    - 1 g red

BRACELET #8
Length: 16"/6.3 cm
Width: 0.6"/1.4 cm

Materials:
- 8 warp threads (cotton thread)
- 10° seed beads:
    - 3 g beige
    - 2 g black
    - 1 g white
    - 1 g yellow
    - 1 g red

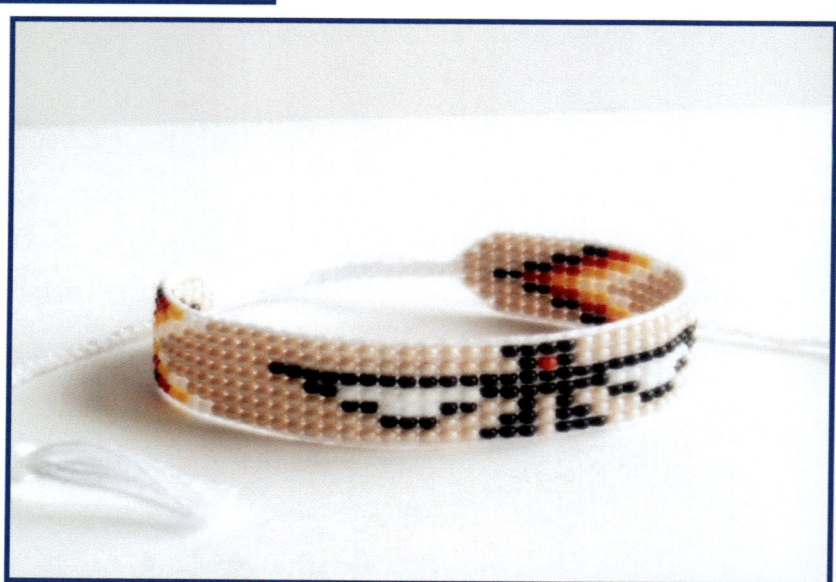

BRACELET #9
Length: 6.5"/16.5 cm
Width: 0.8"/2 cm

Materials:
- 12 warp threads (cotton thread)
- 10° seed beads:
    - 6 g beige
    - 2 g black
    - 1 g white
    - 1 g yellow
    - 1 g red

9

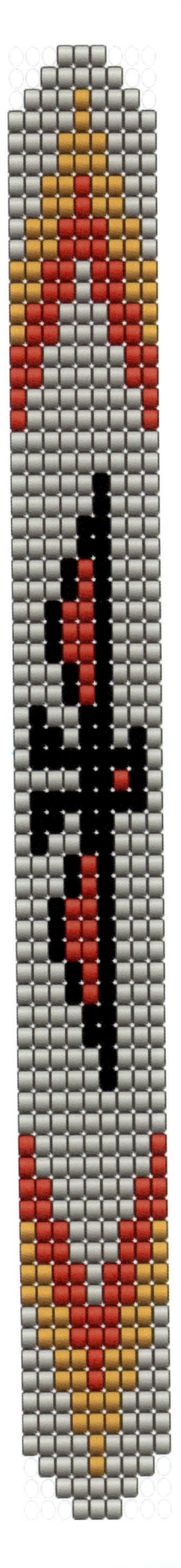

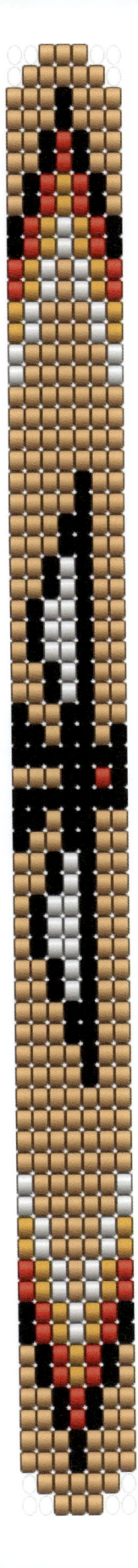

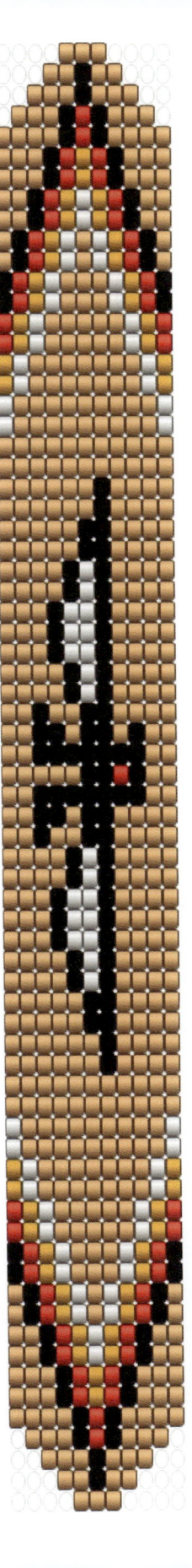

BRACELET #10
Length: 6.7"/17 cm
Width: 0.8"/2 cm

Materials:
- 12 warp threads (embroidery threads)
- 10° seed beads:
  - 5 g deep blue
  - 2 g white
  - 1 g yellow
  - 2 g red

BRACELET #11
Length: 6.3"/16 cm
Width: 0.7"/1.7 cm

Materials:
- 10 warp threads (embroidery
- 10° seed beads:
  - 4 g deep blue
  - 2 g white
  - 2 g red

BRACELET #12
Length: 7.3"/18.5 cm
Width: 0.9"/2.3 cm

Materials:
- 14 warp threads (embroidery threads)
- 10° seed beads:
  - 6 g deep blue
  - 3 g white
  - 3 g red

11

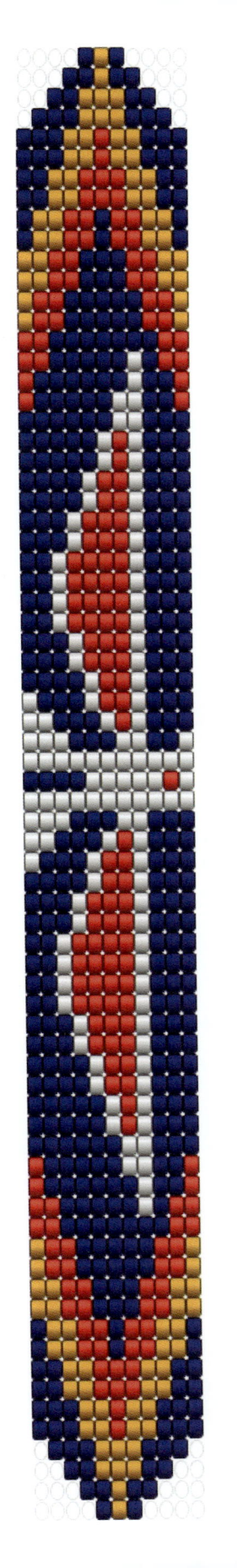

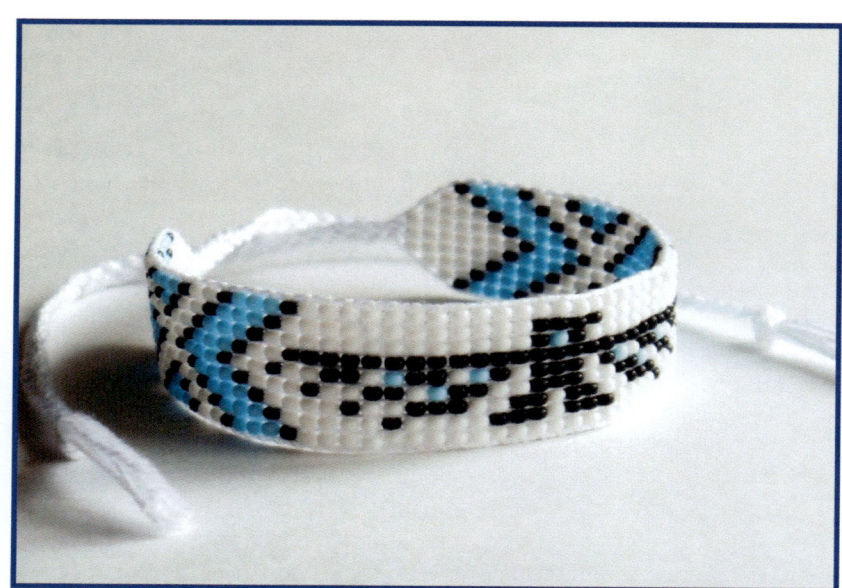

BRACELET #13
Length: 6.3"/16 cm
Width: 0.7"/1.7 cm

Materials:
- 10 warp threads (cotton thread)
- 10° seed beads:
    - 4 g white
    - 2 g black
    - 2 g blue

BRACELET #14
Length: 6.9"/17.5 cm
Width: 0.8"/2 cm

Materials:
- 12 warp threads (cotton thread)
- 10° seed beads:
    - 5 g white
    - 3 g black
    - 2 g red

BRACELET #15
Length: 7.5"/19 cm
Width: 0.8"/2 cm

Materials:
- 12 warp threads (cotton thread)
- 10° seed beads:
    - 5 g white
    - 3 g black
    - 1 g yellow
    - 2 g red

13

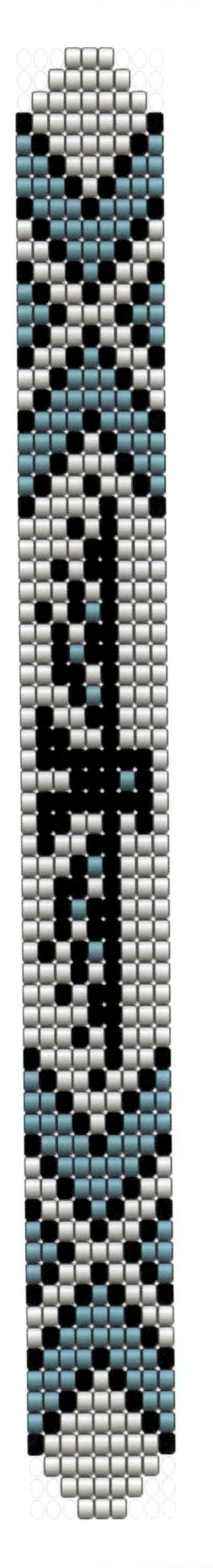

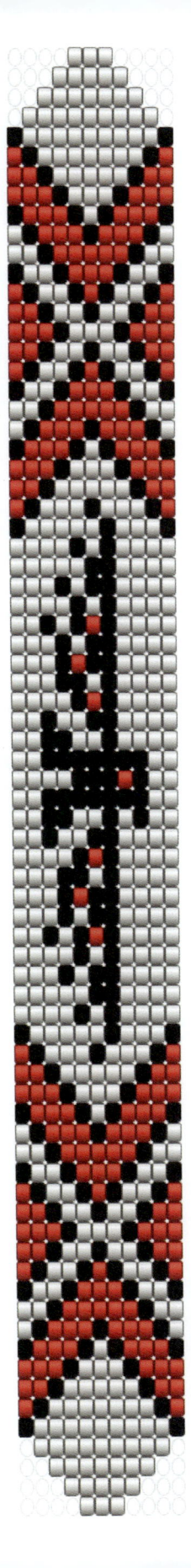

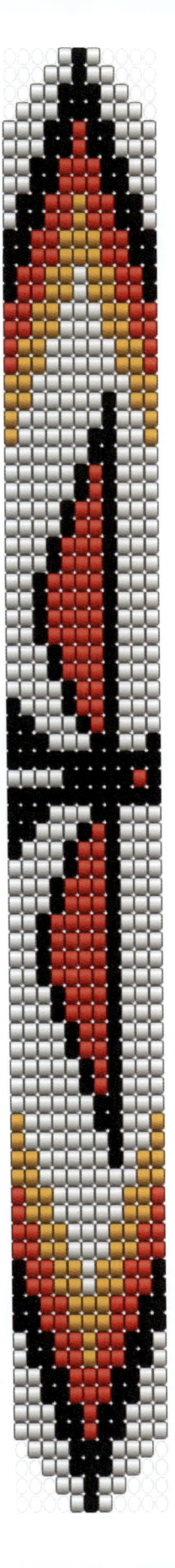

BRACELET #16
Length: 7.1"/18 cm
Width: 0.9"/2.3 cm

Materials:
- 14 warp threads (cotton thread)
- 10° seed beads:
  - 6 g black
  - 2 g white
  - 1 g light yellow
  - 1 g yellow
  - 1 g orange
  - 2 g red

BRACELET #17
Length: 7.5"/19 cm
Width: 0.9"/2.3 cm

Materials:
- 14 warp threads (embroidery threads)
- 10° seed beads:
  - 6 g red
  - 2 g black
  - 2 g white
  - 1 g light yellow
  - 1 g yellow
  - 1 g orange

BRACELET #18
Length: 7.5"/19 cm
Width: 0.9"/2.3 cm

Materials:
- 14 warp threads (cotton thread)
- 10° seed beads:
  - 6 g beige
  - 2 g black
  - 2 g white
  - 1 g light yellow
  - 1 g yellow
  - 1 g orange
  - 1 g red

15

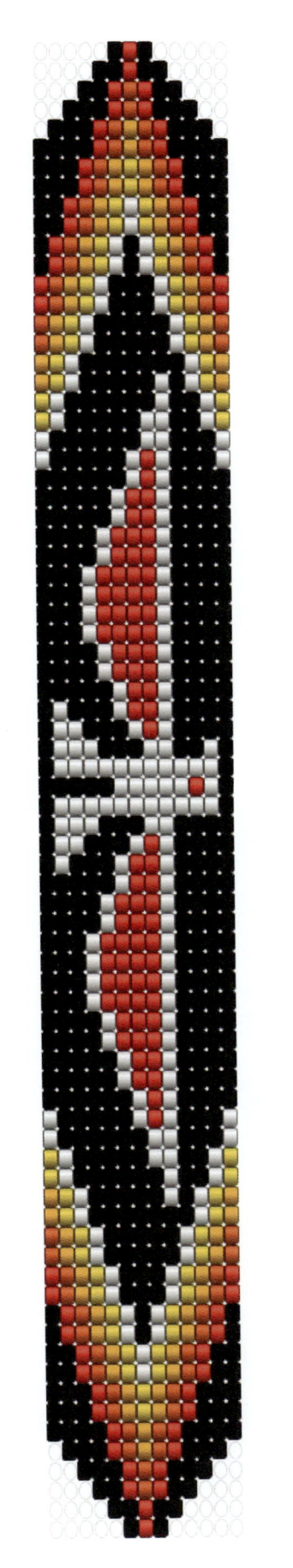

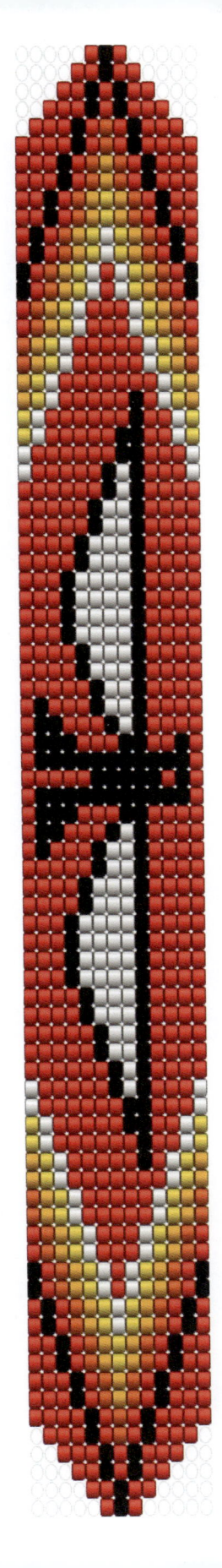

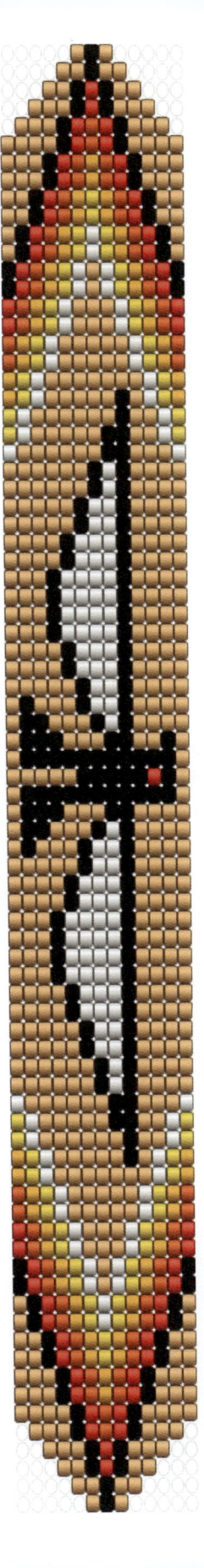

BRACELET #19
Length: 6.1"/15.5 cm
Width: 0.6"/1.4 cm

Materials:
- 8 warp threads (embroidery threads)
- 10° seed beads:
    - 3 g deep blue
    - 1 g red
    - 1 g yellow
    - 1 g green
    - 1 g blue

BRACELET #20
Length: 6.5"/16.5 cm
Width: 0.7"/1.7 cm

Materials:
- 10 warp threads (cotton thread)
- 10° seed beads:
    - 5 g crystal silver lined
    - 2 g red
    - 1 g yellow
    - 1 g black

BRACELET #21
Length: 6.5"/16.5 cm
Width: 0.8"/2 cm

Materials:
- 12 warp threads (cotton thread)
- 10° seed beads:
    - 6 g black
    - 1 g crystal silver lined
    - 1 g light yellow
    - 1 g yellow
    - 1 g orange
    - 1 g red

17

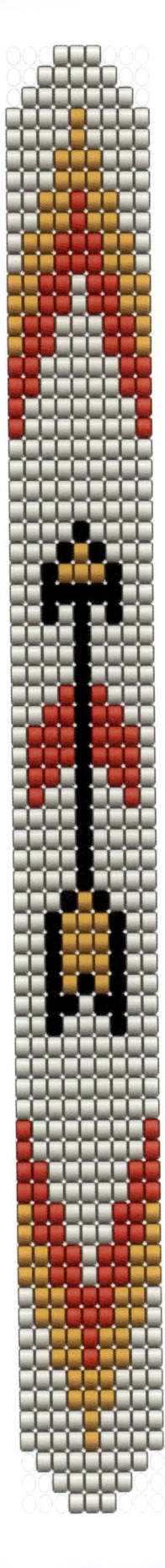

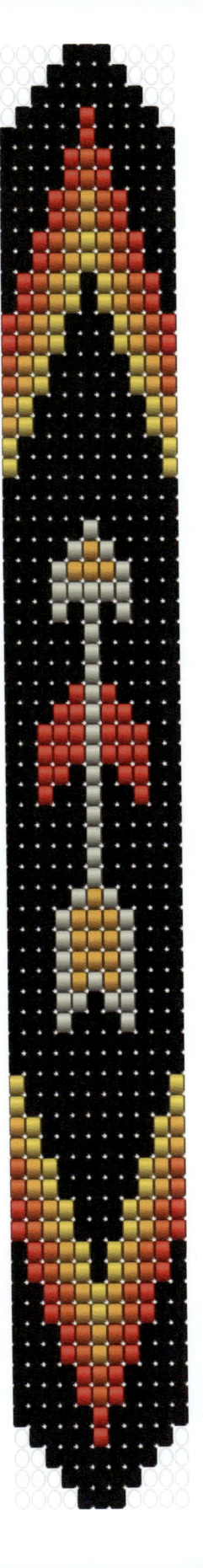

BRACELET #22
Length: 6.1"/15.5 cm
Width: 0.9"/2.3 cm

Materials:
- 14 warp threads (cotton thread)
- 10° seed beads:
  - 6 g black
  - 3 g grey silver lined
  - 2 g white
  - 1 g blue

BRACELET #23
Length: 4.9"/12.5 cm
Full length (with bars): 6.5"/16.5 cm
Width: 1.1"/2.9 cm

Materials:
- 18 warp threads (beading thread)
- 10° seed beads:
  - 6 g black
  - 3 g grey silver lined
  - 3 g white
  - 1 g blue
- 2 pieces of leather 1.6"*1.2"/4*3 cm
- 2 5 mm metal eyelets with washers
- 2 suede cords 15.7"/40 cm long

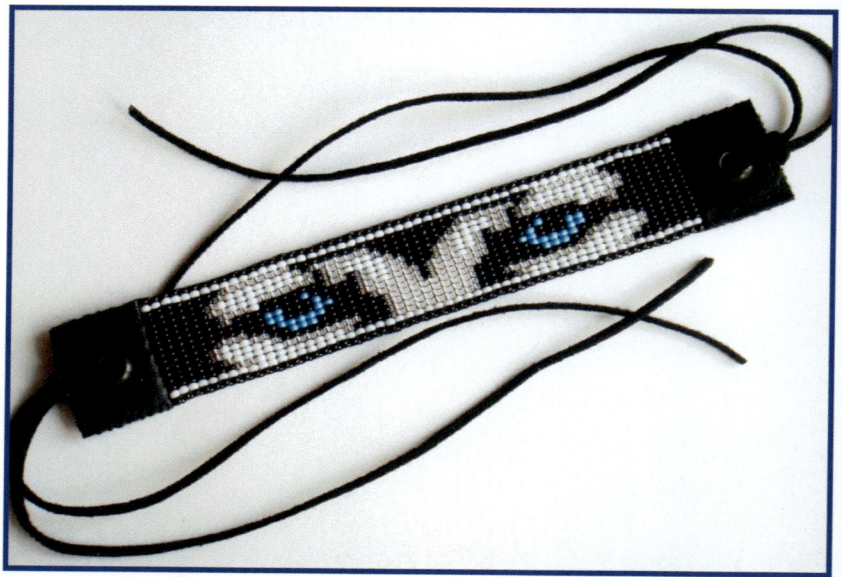

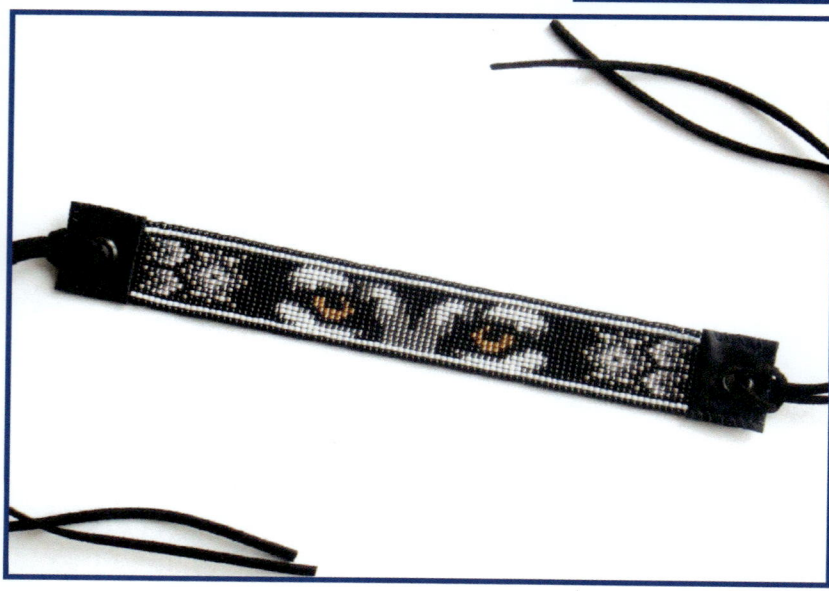

BRACELET #24
Length: 5.7"/14.6 cm
Full length (with bars): 7.3"/18.6 cm
Width: 0.9"/2.4 cm

Materials:
- 18 warp threads (beading thread)
- 15° seed beads:
  - 3 g black   1 g hematite
  - 2 g white   1 g grey silver lined
  - 1 g yellow   1 g light grey silver lined
  - 1 g silver   1 g crystal silver lined
- 2 pieces of leather 1.6"*1"/4*2.5 cm
- 2 5 mm metal eyelets with washers
- 2 suede cords 15.7"/40 cm long

19

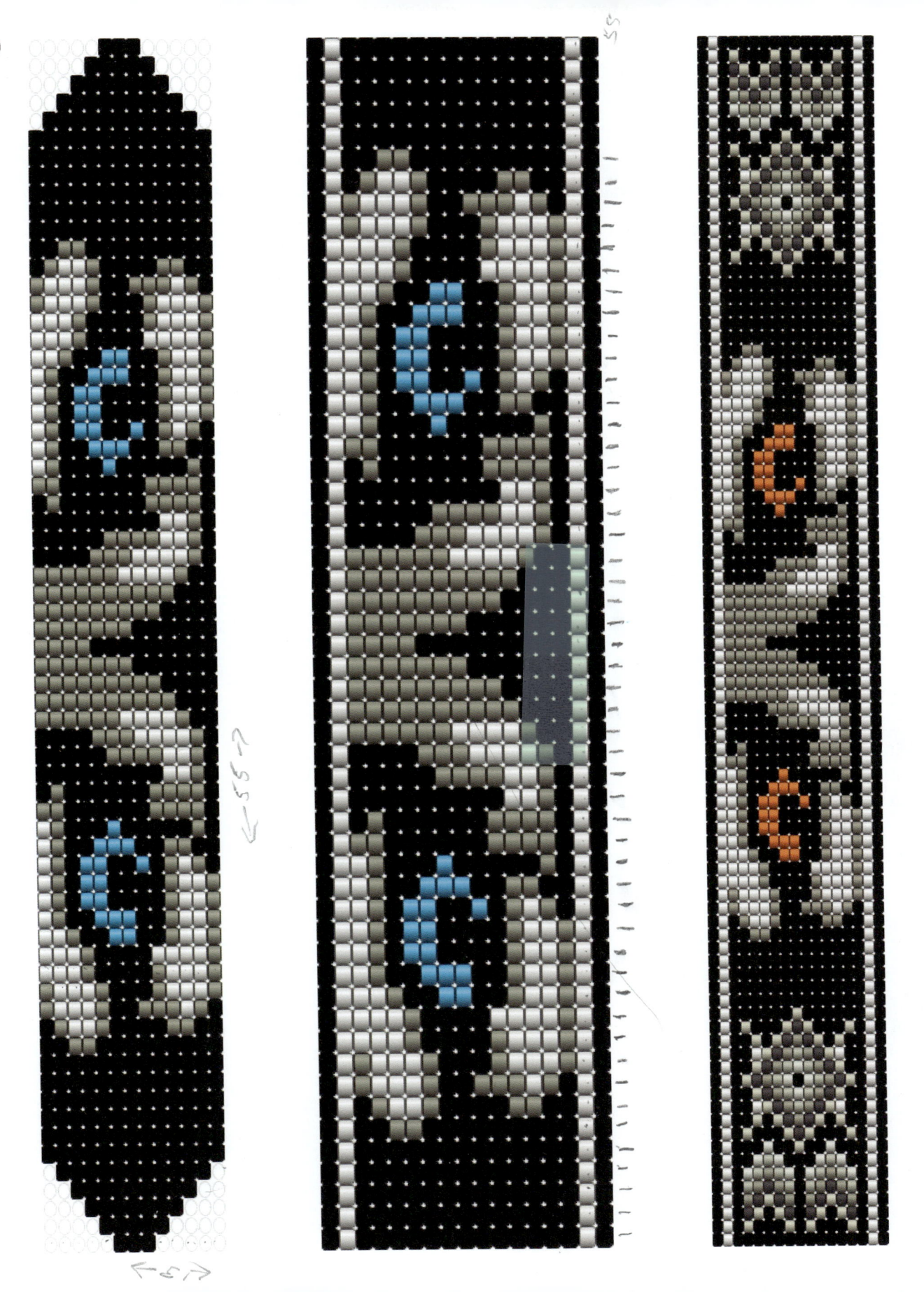

20

BRACELET #25
Length: 5.9"/15 cm
Width: 0.9"/2.3 cm

Materials:
- 14 warp threads (cotton thread)
- 10° seed beads:
    - 5 g white
    - 1 g black
    - 1 g red
    - 1 g orange
    - 1 g yellow
    - 1 g light yellow

BRACELET #26
Length: 5.9"/15 cm
Width: 1"/2.6 cm

Materials:
- 16 warp threads (cotton thread)
- 10° seed beads:
    - 5 g beige
    - 1 g black
    - 1 g white
    - 1 g light yellow
    - 1 g yellow
    - 1 g orange
    - 1 g red

BRACELET #27
Length: 6.9"/17.5 cm
Width: 1.3"/3.4 cm

Materials:
- 22 warp threads (embroidery threads)
- 10° seed beads:
    - 6 g brown
    - 2 g red
    - 4 g orange
    - 5 g yellow
    - 1 g white

21

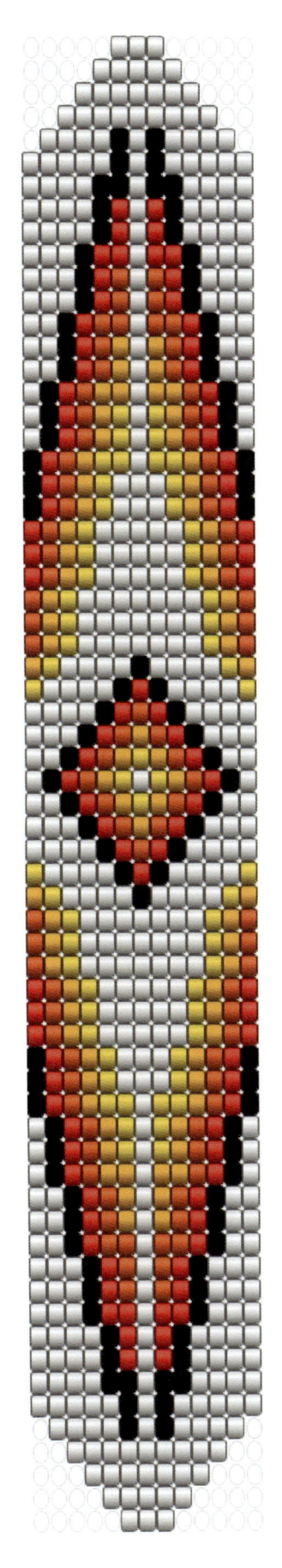

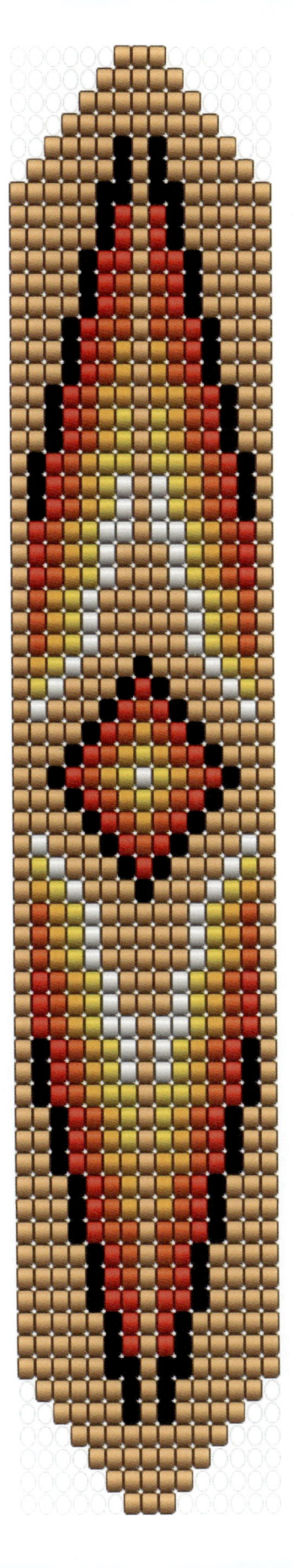

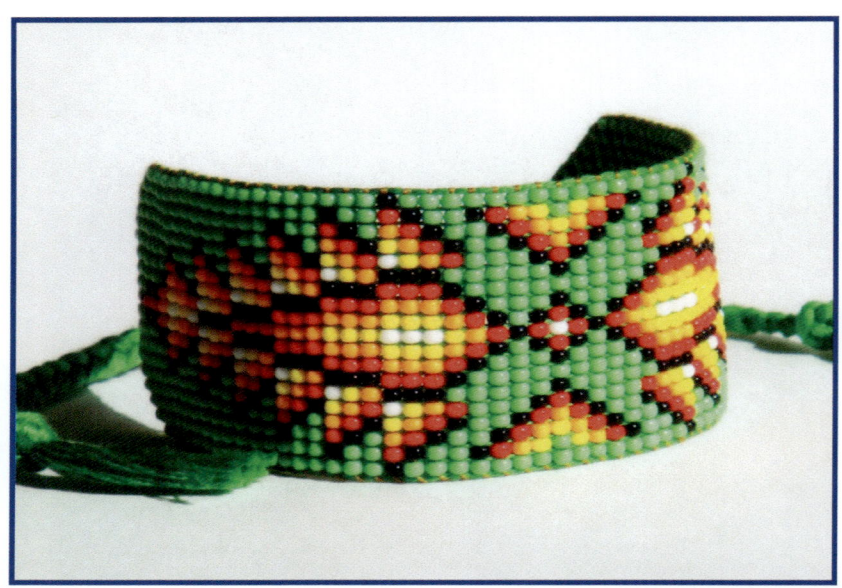

BRACELET #28
Length: 6.1"/15.5 cm
Width: 1.2"/3.1 cm

Materials:
- 20 warp threads (embroidery threads)
- 10° seed beads:
  - 7 g green
  - 2 g black
  - 1 g white
  - 1 g yellow
  - 2 g orange
  - 2 g red

BRACELET #29
Length: 6.1"/15.5 cm
Width: 1.2"/3.1 cm

Materials:
- 20 warp threads (embroidery threads)
- 10° seed beads:
  - 7 g blue
  - 2 g black
  - 1 g white
  - 1 g yellow
  - 2 g orange
  - 2 g red

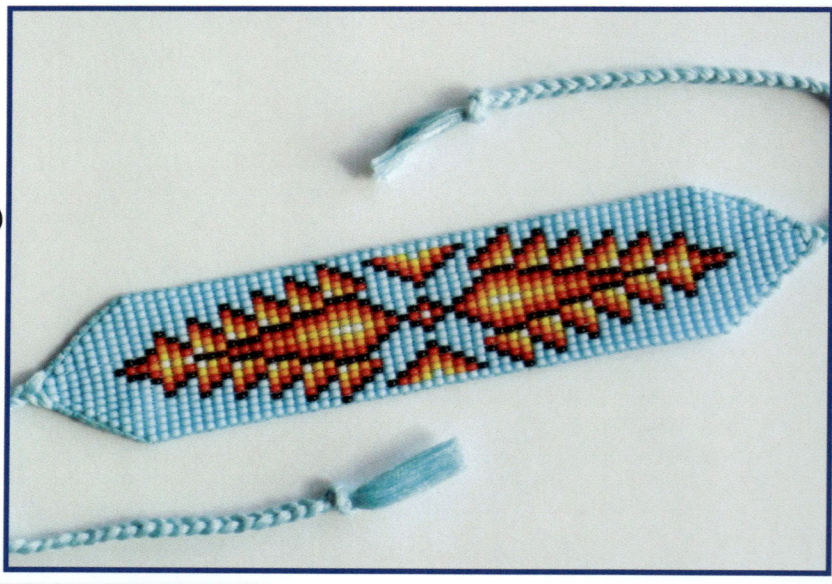

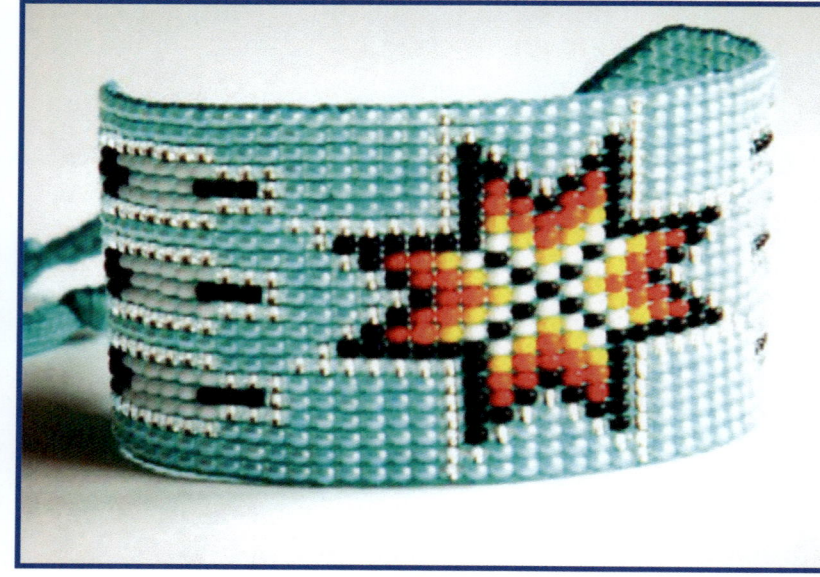

BRACELET #30
Length: 6.1"/15.5 cm
Width: 1.3"/3.4 cm

Materials:
- 22 warp threads (embroidery threads)
- 10° seed beads:
  - 8 g blue
  - 2 g black
  - 1 g red
  - 1 g orange
  - 1 g yellow
  - 2 g white
  - 3 g crystal silver lined

23

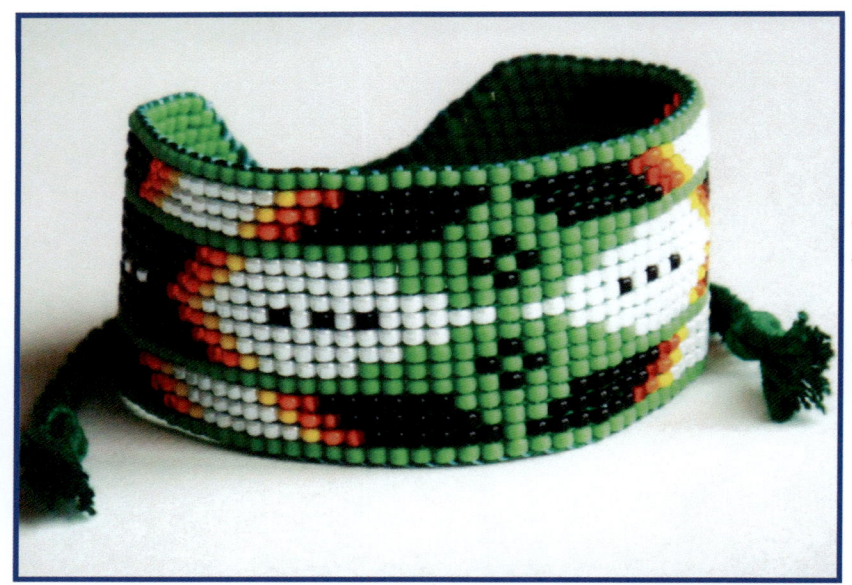

BRACELET #31
Length: 6.7"/17 cm
Width: 1.1"/2.9 cm

Materials:
- 18 warp threads (embroidery threads)
- 10° seed beads:
    - 6 g green
    - 4 g black
    - 3 g white
    - 1 g yellow
    - 1 g orange
    - 1 g red

BRACELET #32
Length: 6.7"/17 cm
Width: 1.1"/2.9 cm

Materials:
- 18 warp threads (embroidery threads)
- 10° seed beads:
    - 6 g blue
    - 4 g black
    - 3 g white
    - 1 g yellow
    - 1 g orange
    - 1 g red

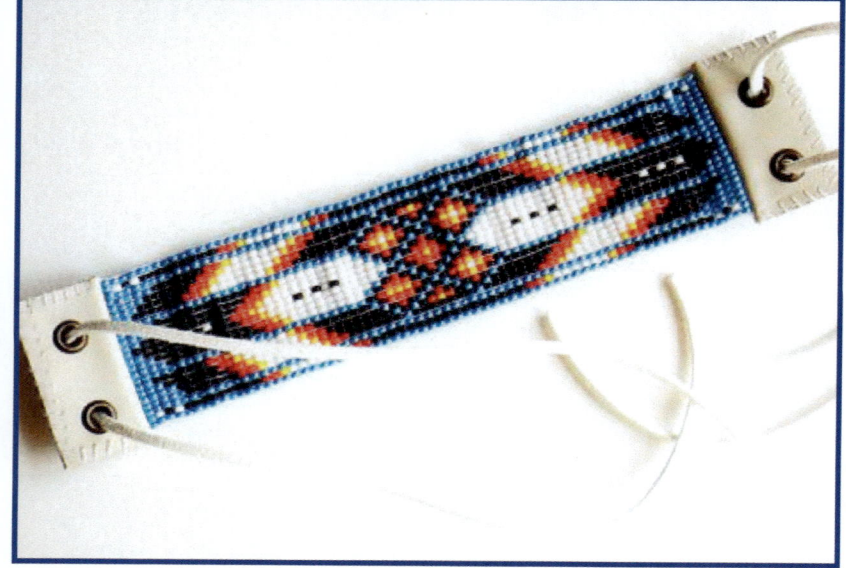

BRACELET #33
Length: 6.1"/15.5 cm
Full length (with bars): 7.7"/19.5 cm
Width: 1.4"/3.7 cm

Materials:
- 24 warp threads (beading thread)
- 10° seed beads:
    - 6 g blue   1 g yellow
    - 6 g black   1 g orange
    - 4 g white   1 g red
- 2 pieces of leather 1.6"*1.6"/ 4*4 cm
- 4 5 mm metal eyelets with washers
- 2 suede cords 15.7"/40 cm long

25

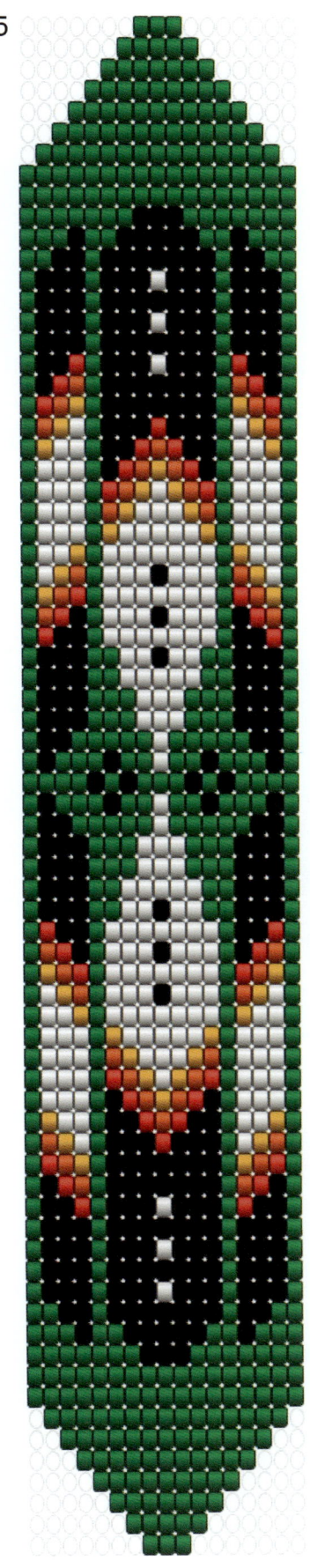

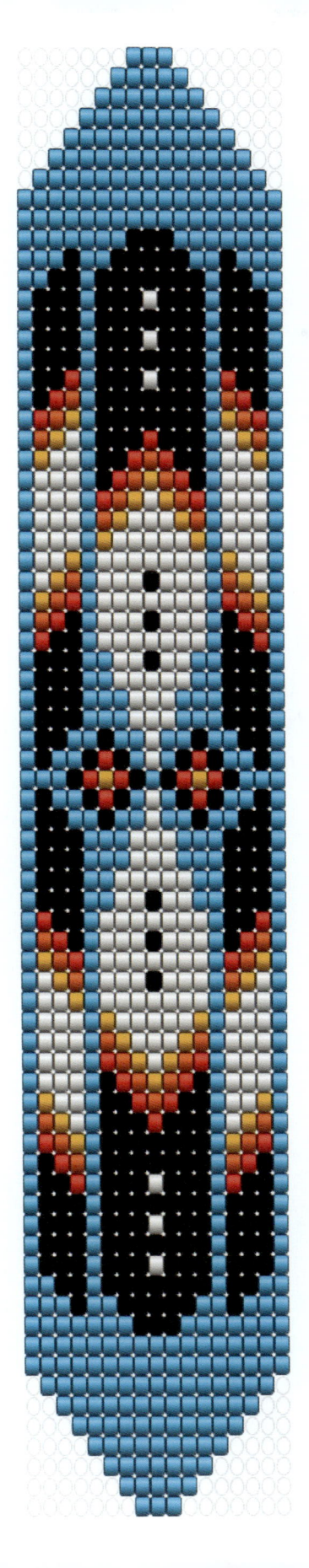

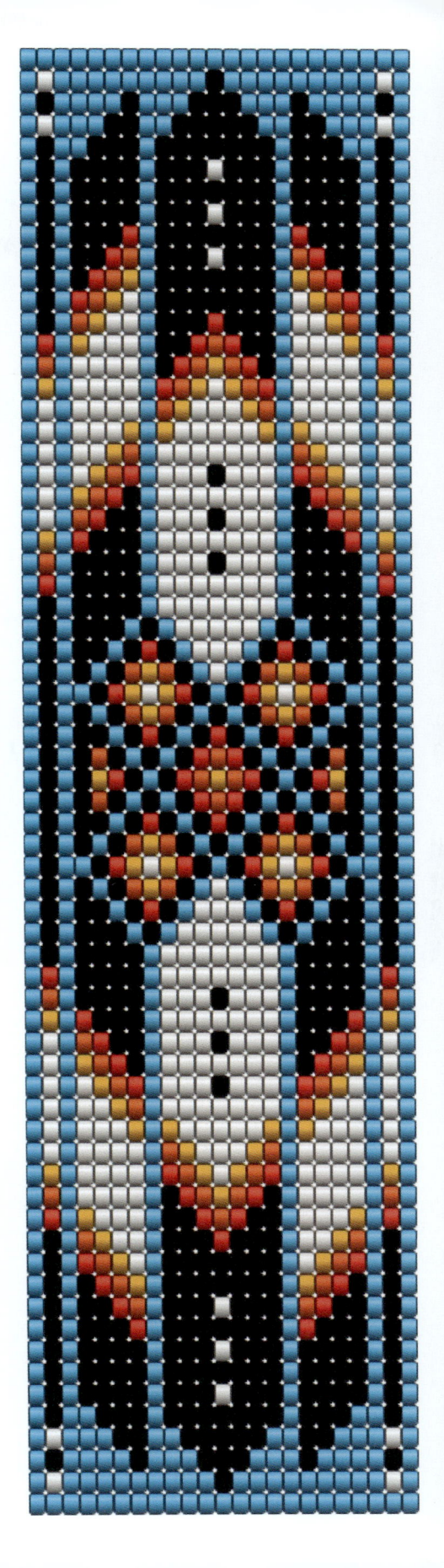

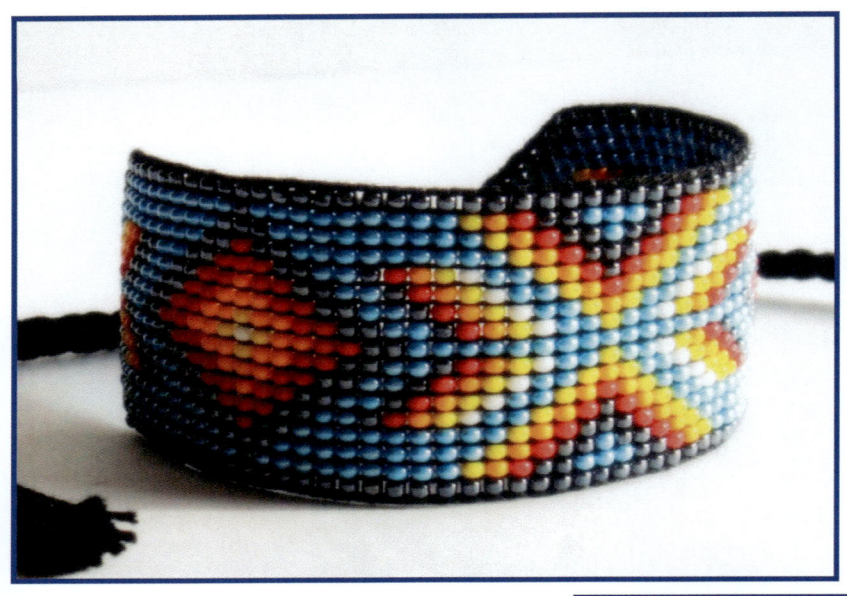

BRACELET #34
Length: 6.1"/15.5 cm
Width: 1.1"/2.9 cm

Materials:
- 18 warp threads (cotton thread)
- 10° seed beads:
    - 5 g blue
    - 4 g hematite
    - 1 g white
    - 1 g yellow
    - 2 g orange
    - 2 g red

BRACELET #35
Length: 6.1"/15.5 cm
Width: 1.1"/2.9 cm

Materials:
- 18 warp threads (embroidery threads)
- 10° seed beads:
    - 7 g blue
    - 2 g black
    - 1 g white
    - 1 g yellow
    - 2 g orange
    - 2 g red

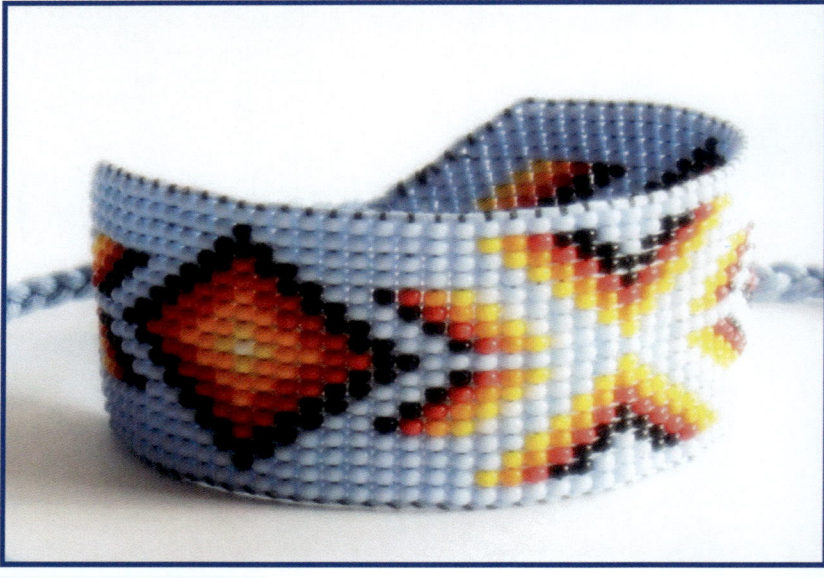

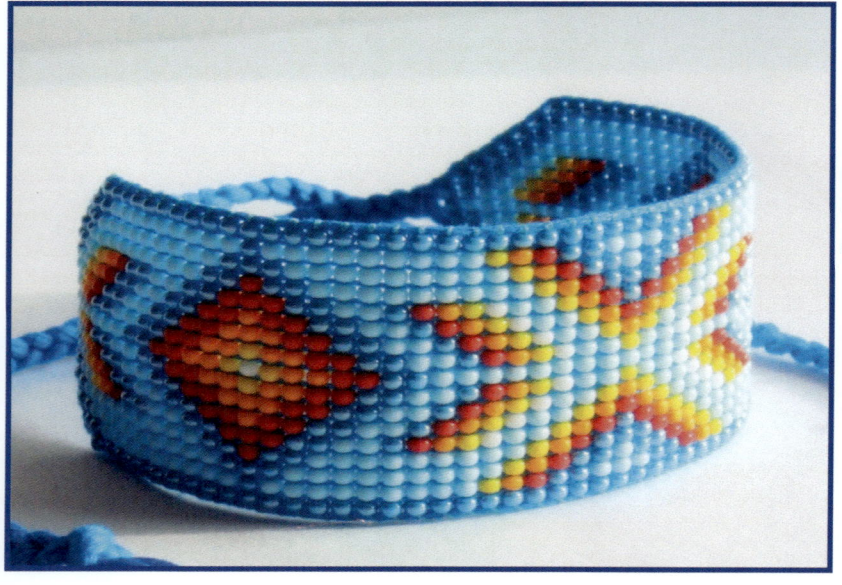

BRACELET #36
Length: 6.1"/15.5 cm
Width: 1.1"/2.9 cm

Materials:
- 18 warp threads (embroidery threads)
- 10° seed beads:
    - 5 g light blue
    - 4 g blue
    - 1 g white
    - 1 g yellow
    - 2 g orange
    - 2 g red

27

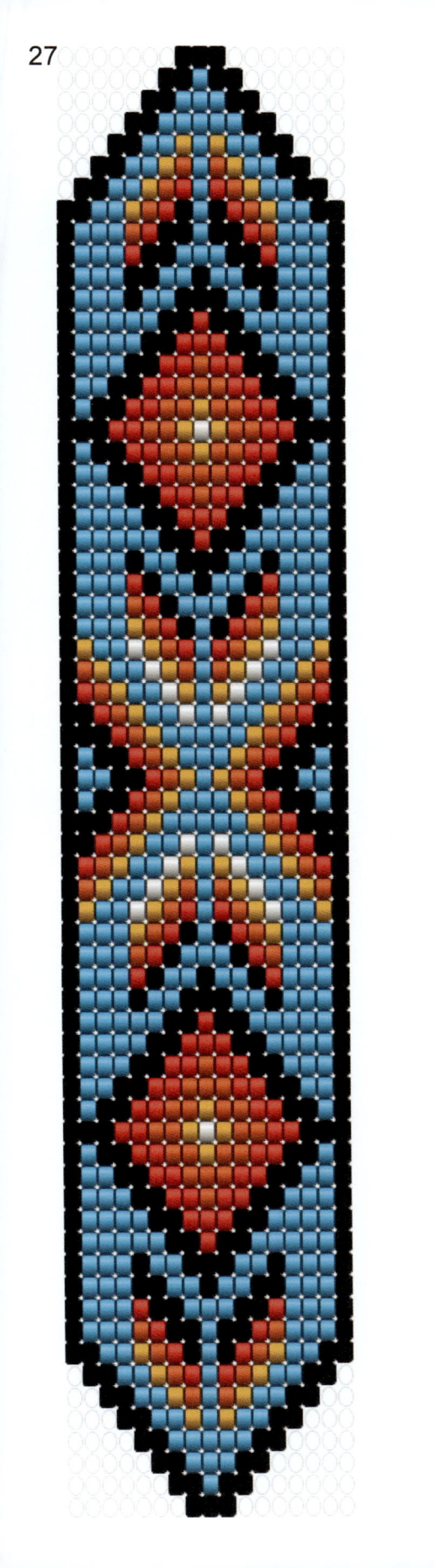

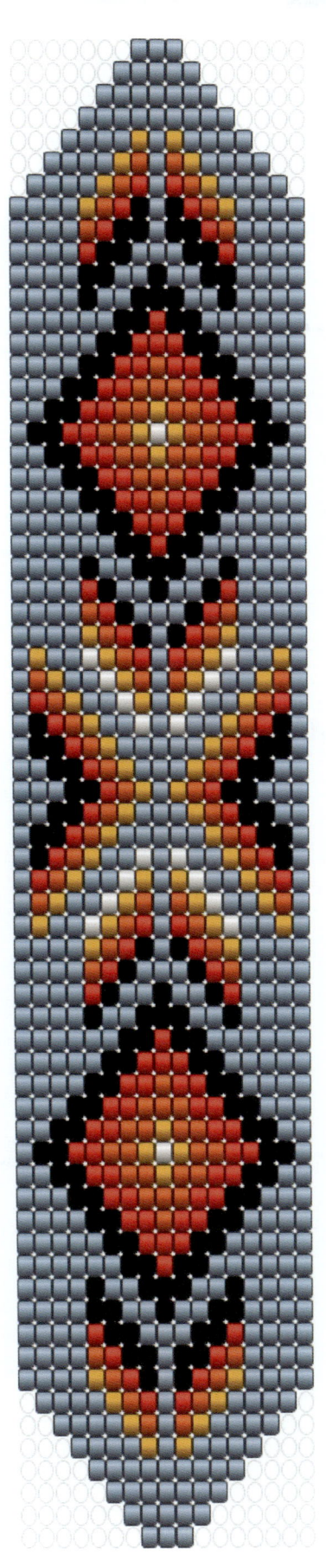

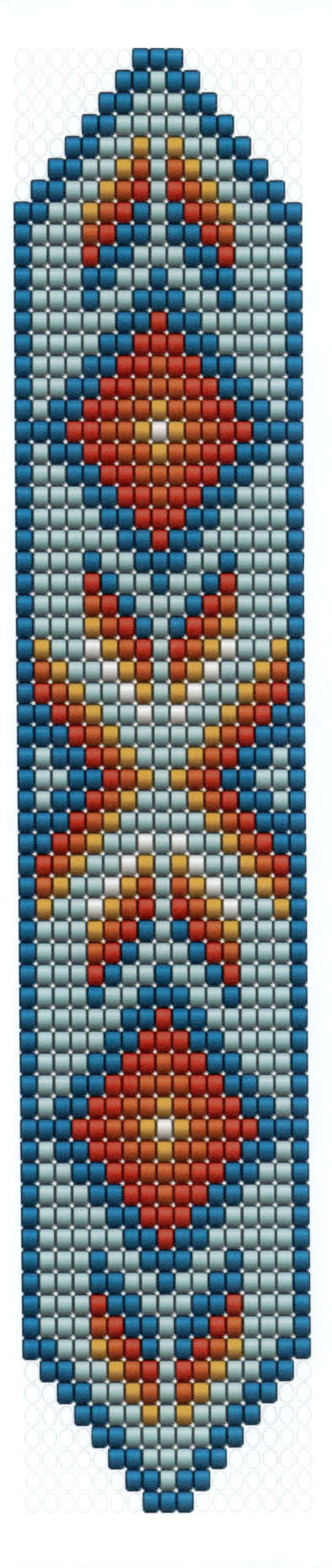

28

BRACELET #37
Length: 6.2"/15.7 cm
Width: 0.8"/2 cm

Materials:
- 12 warp threads (embroidery threads)
- 10° seed beads:
    - 4 g blue
    - 1 g black
    - 1 g white
    - 2 g yellow
    - 1 g orange
    - 2 g red

BRACELET #38
Length: 6.4"/16.3 cm
Width: 1"/2.6 cm

Materials:
- 16 warp threads (embroidery threads)
- 10° seed beads:
    - 6 g blue
    - 2 g black
    - 2 g white
    - 1 g yellow
    - 1 g orange
    - 1 g red

BRACELET #39
Length: 5.7"/14.5 cm
Full length (with bars): 7.3"/18.5 cm
Width: 0.9"/2.3 cm

Materials:
- 14 warp threads (beading thread)
- 10° seed beads:
    - 2 g blue   2 g yellow
    - 2 g black   2 g orange
    - 1 g white   2 g red
- 2 pieces of leather 1.6"*1"/ 4*2.5 cm
- 2 5 mm metal eyelets with washers
- 2 suede cords 15.7"/40 cm long

29

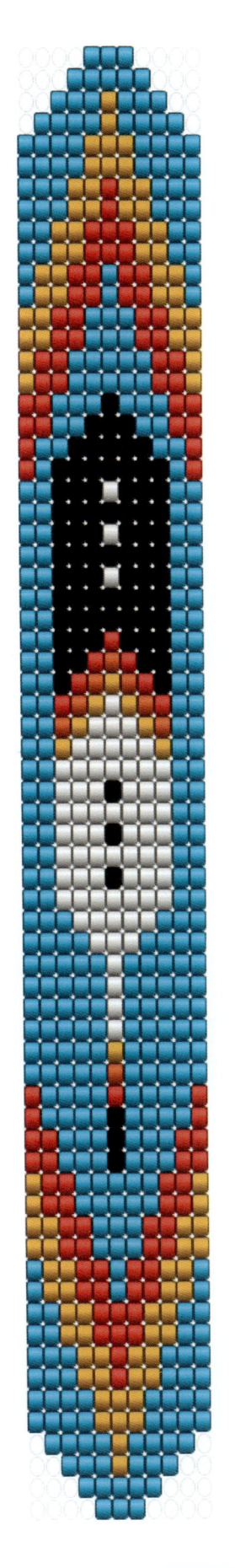

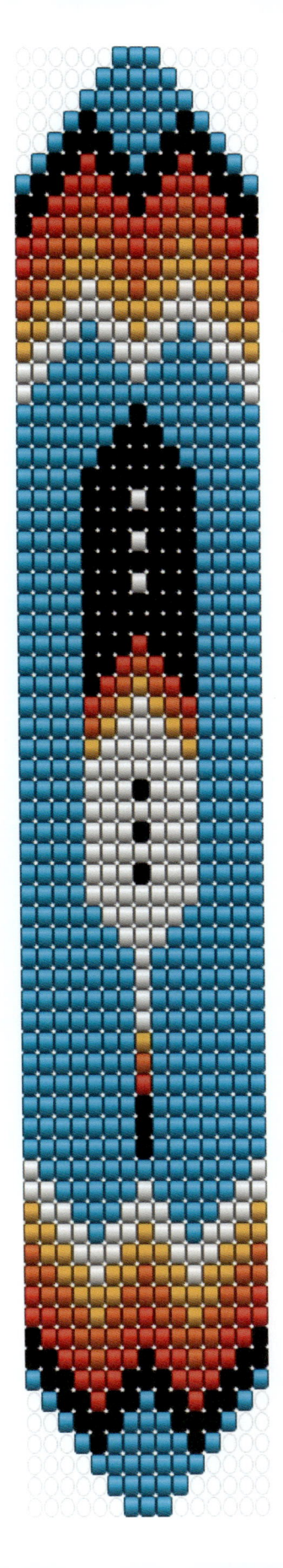

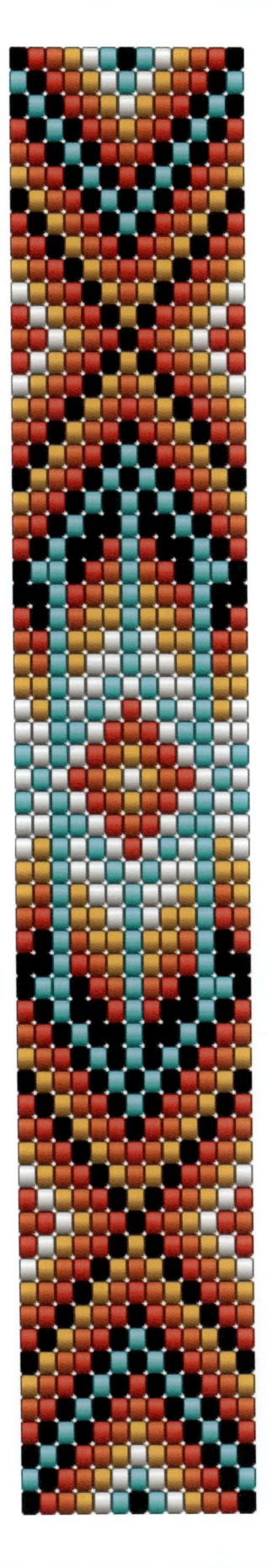

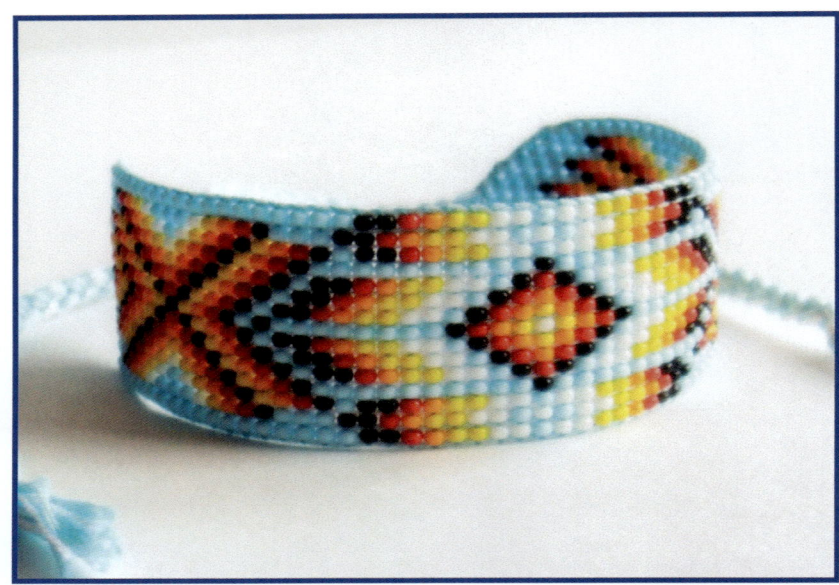

BRACELET #40
Length: 6.1"/15.5 cm
Width: 1"/2.6 cm

Materials:
- 16 warp threads (embroidery threads)
- 10° seed beads:
  - 4 g blue
  - 2 g black
  - 1 g white
  - 2 g yellow
  - 2 g orange
  - 2 g red

BRACELET #41
Length: 6.1"/15.5 cm
Width: 0.9"/2.3 cm

Materials:
- 14 warp threads (cotton thread)
- 10° seed beads:
  - 3 g blue
  - 2 g black
  - 1 g white
  - 1 g yellow
  - 2 g orange
  - 2 g red

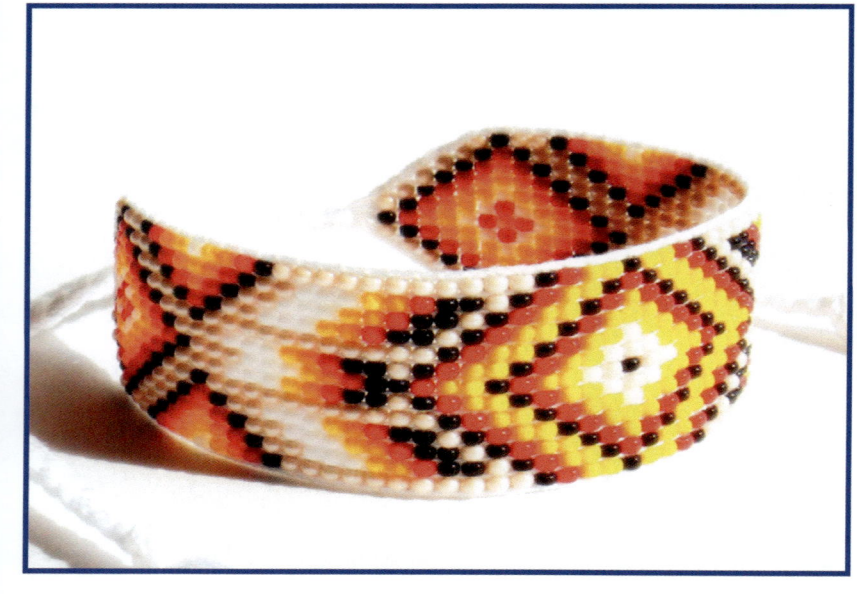

BRACELET #42
Length: 6.1"/15.5 cm
Width: 0.9"/2.3 cm

Materials:
- 14 warp threads (cotton thread)
- 10° seed beads:
  - 3 g beige
  - 2 g black
  - 1 g white
  - 1 g yellow
  - 2 g orange
  - 2 g red

31

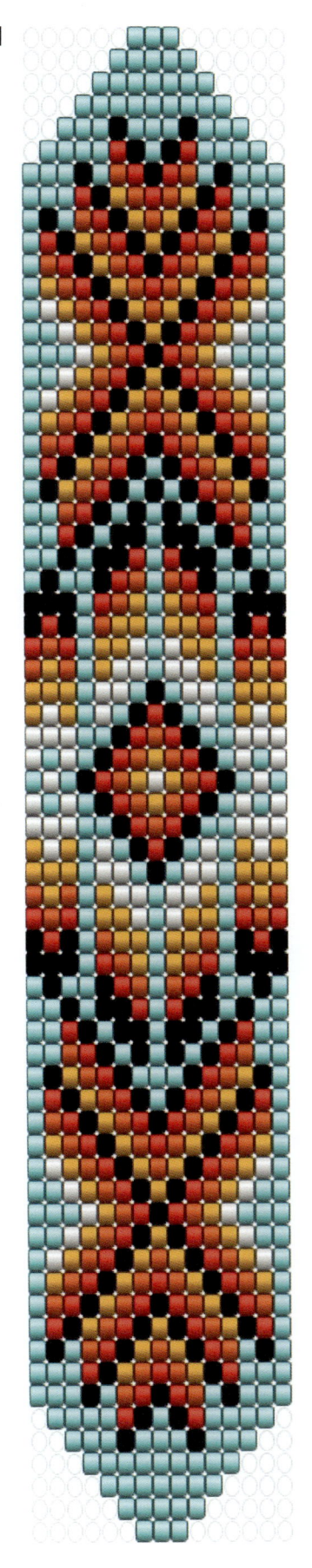

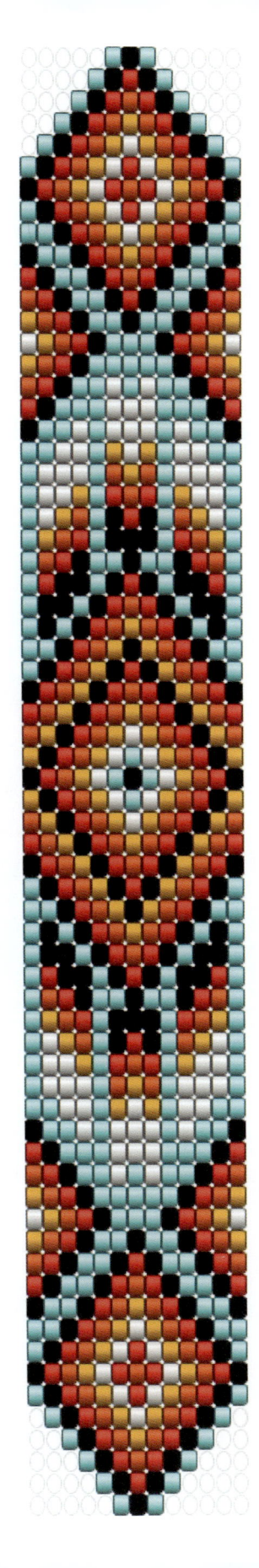

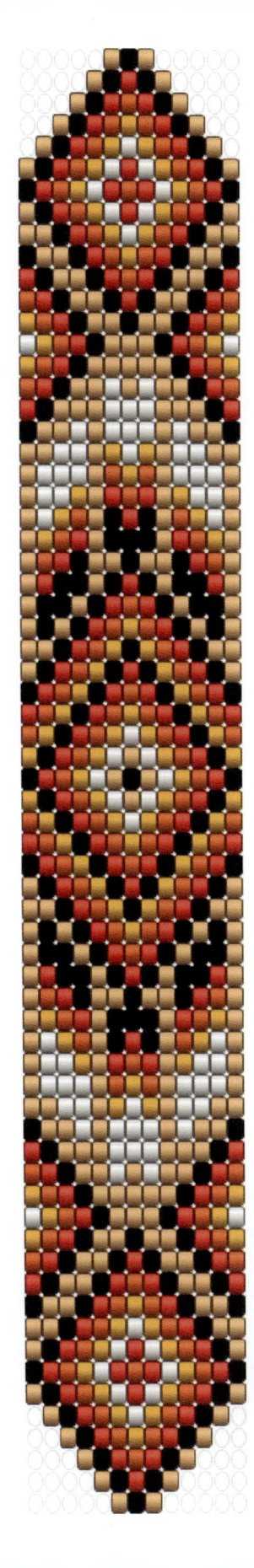

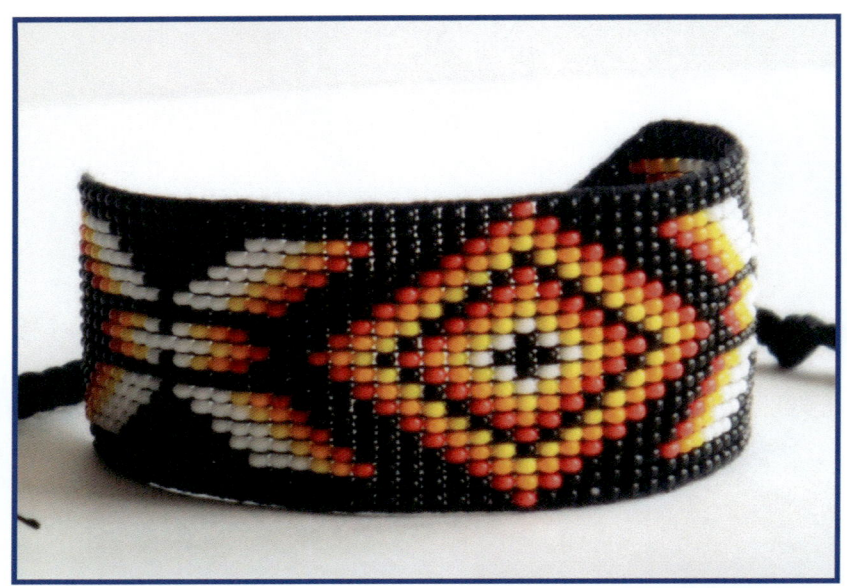

BRACELET #43
Length: 6.3"/16 cm
Width: 1.2"/3.1 cm

Materials:
- 20 warp threads (cotton thread)
- 10° seed beads:
  - 8 g black
  - 2 g white
  - 1 g yellow
  - 2 g orange
  - 2 g red

BRACELET #44
Length: 6.1"/15.5 cm
Width: 1.3"/3.4 cm

Materials:
- 22 warp threads (embroidery threads)
- 10° seed beads:
  - 8 g blue
  - 3 g black
  - 3 g white
  - 1 g yellow
  - 1 g orange
  - 1 g red

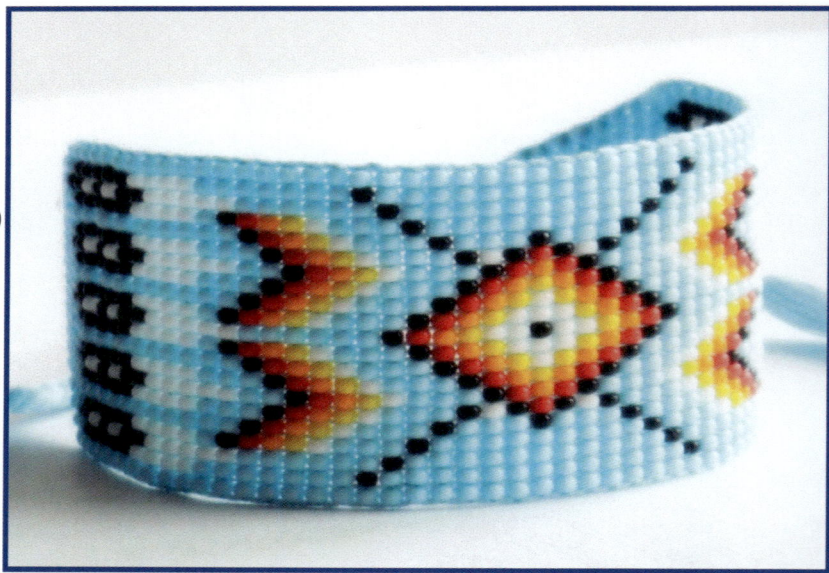

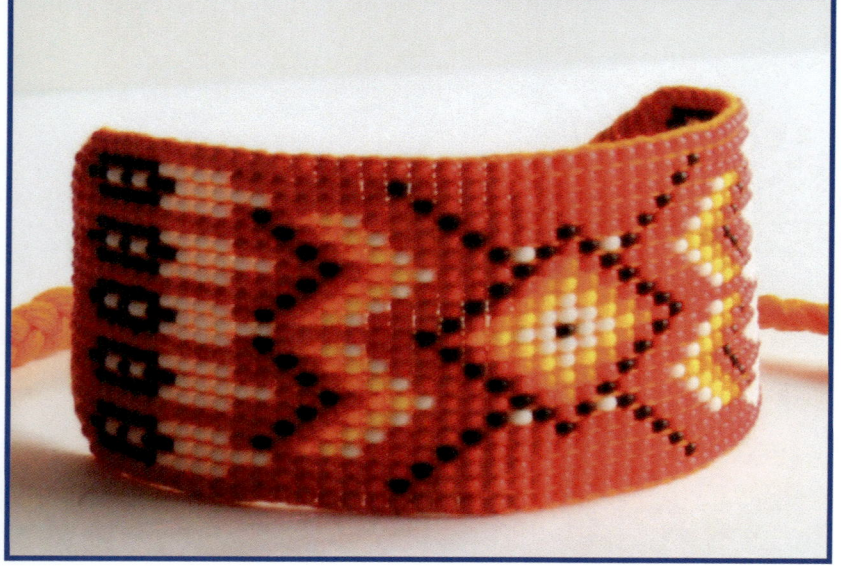

BRACELET #45
Length: 6.1"/15.5 cm
Width: 1.3"/3.4 cm

Materials:
- 22 warp threads (embroidery threads)
- 10° seed beads:
  - 8 g red
  - 1 g orange
  - 1 g yellow
  - 3 g white
  - 3 g black

33

34

BRACELET #46
Length: 6.1"/15.5 cm
Width: 1"/2.6 cm

Materials:
- 16 warp threads (embroidery threads)
- 10° seed beads:
    - 6 g red
    - 1 g orange
    - 1 g yellow
    - 1 g white
    - 3 g black

BRACELET #47
Length: 6.1"/15.5 cm
Width: 1"/2.6 cm

Materials:
- 16 warp threads (embroidery threads)
- 10° seed beads:
    - 6 g orange
    - 1 g yellow
    - 1 g red
    - 3 g black
    - 1 g white

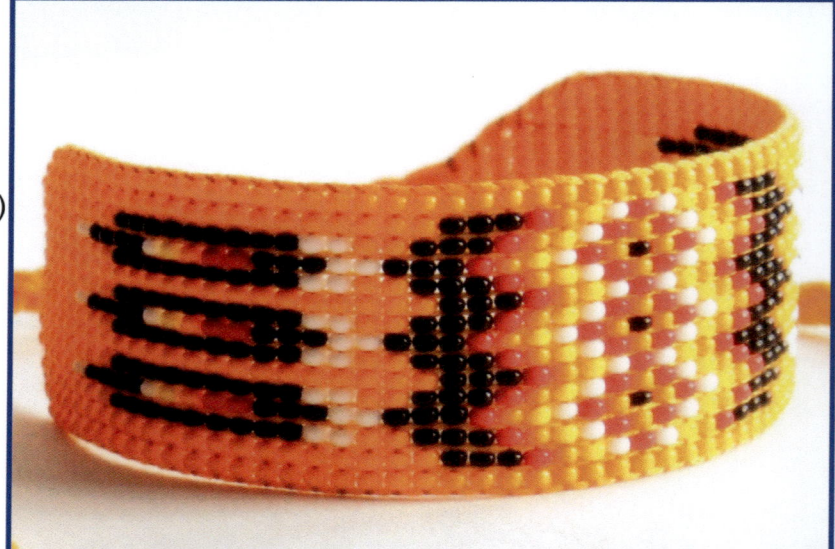

BRACELET #48
Length: 6.1"/15.5 cm
Width: 1"/2.6 cm

Materials:
- 16 warp threads (embroidery threads)
- 10° seed beads:
    - 6 g yellow
    - 1 g orange
    - 1 g red
    - 3 g black
    - 1 g white

35